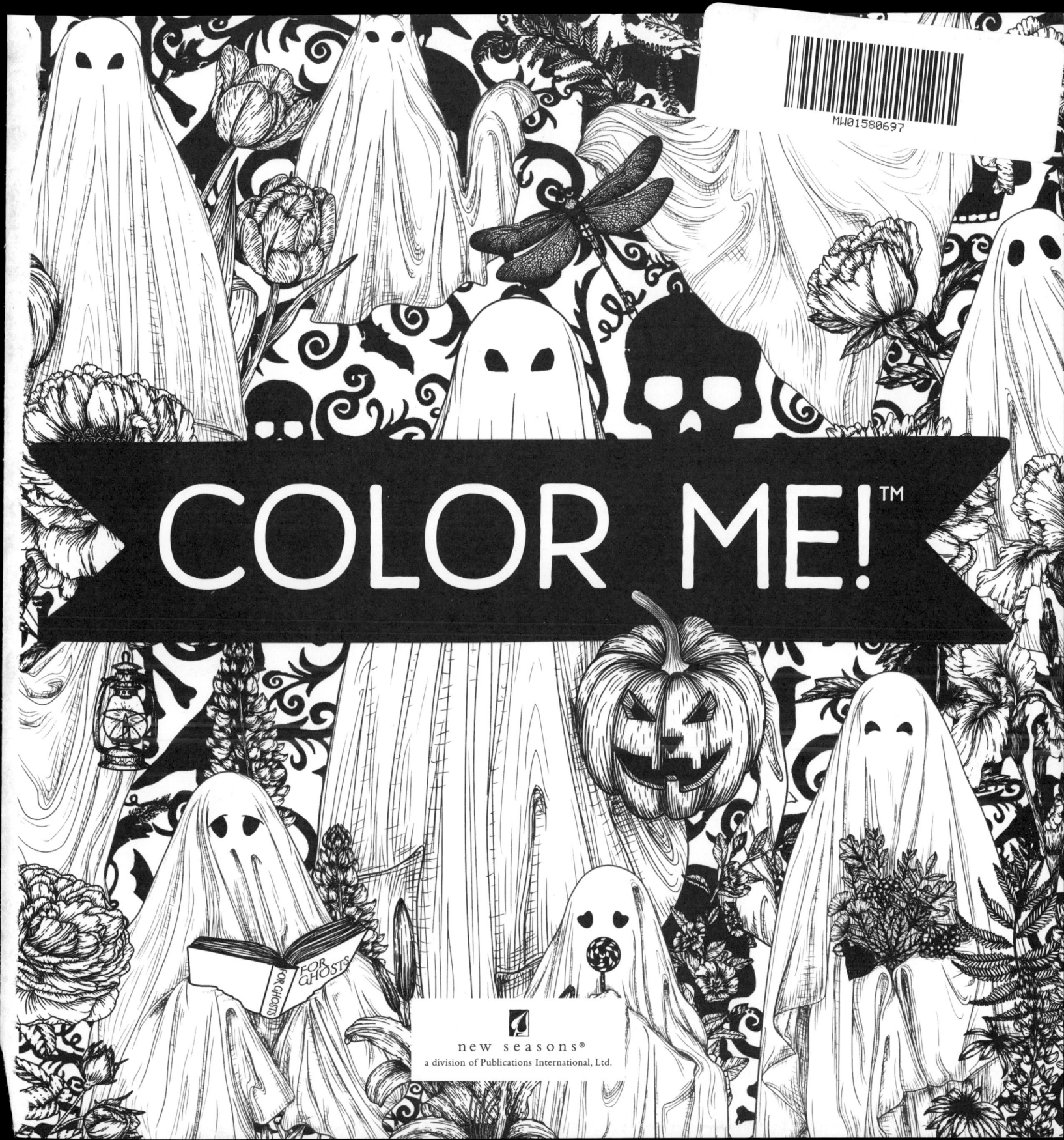

New Seasons is a registered trademark of Publications International, Ltd.
Color Me! is a trademark of Publications International, Ltd.

Copyright © 2025 Publications International, Ltd. All rights reserved.
This book may not be reproduced or quoted in whole or in part by any
means whatsoever without written permission from:

Louis Weber, CEO
Publications International, Ltd.
8140 Lehigh Avenue
Morton Grove, IL 60053

Images from Shutterstock.com

Permission is never granted for commercial purposes.

ISBN: 978-1-63938-843-1

Manufactured in China.

8 7 6 5 4 3 2 1

Let's get social!

 @Publications_International

 @PublicationsInternational

www.pilbooks.com

Thus hath the candle singed the moth.

—William Shakespeare

So many ghosts, and forms of fright,
Have started from their graves to-night.

—Henry Wadsworth Longfellow

I'm so glad I live in a world
where there are Octobers.

—L. M. Montgomery

A Bunch of Hocus Pocus

Then, Autumn, work thy witchery!
Strew the ground with poppy-seeds,
And let my bed be hung with weeds.

—George Parsons Lathrop

SWEET AND SCARY

Double, double toil and trouble;
Fire burn, and cauldron bubble.

—William Shakespeare

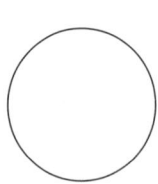

Evil thenceforth became my good.

—Mary Shelley

Candy Inspector

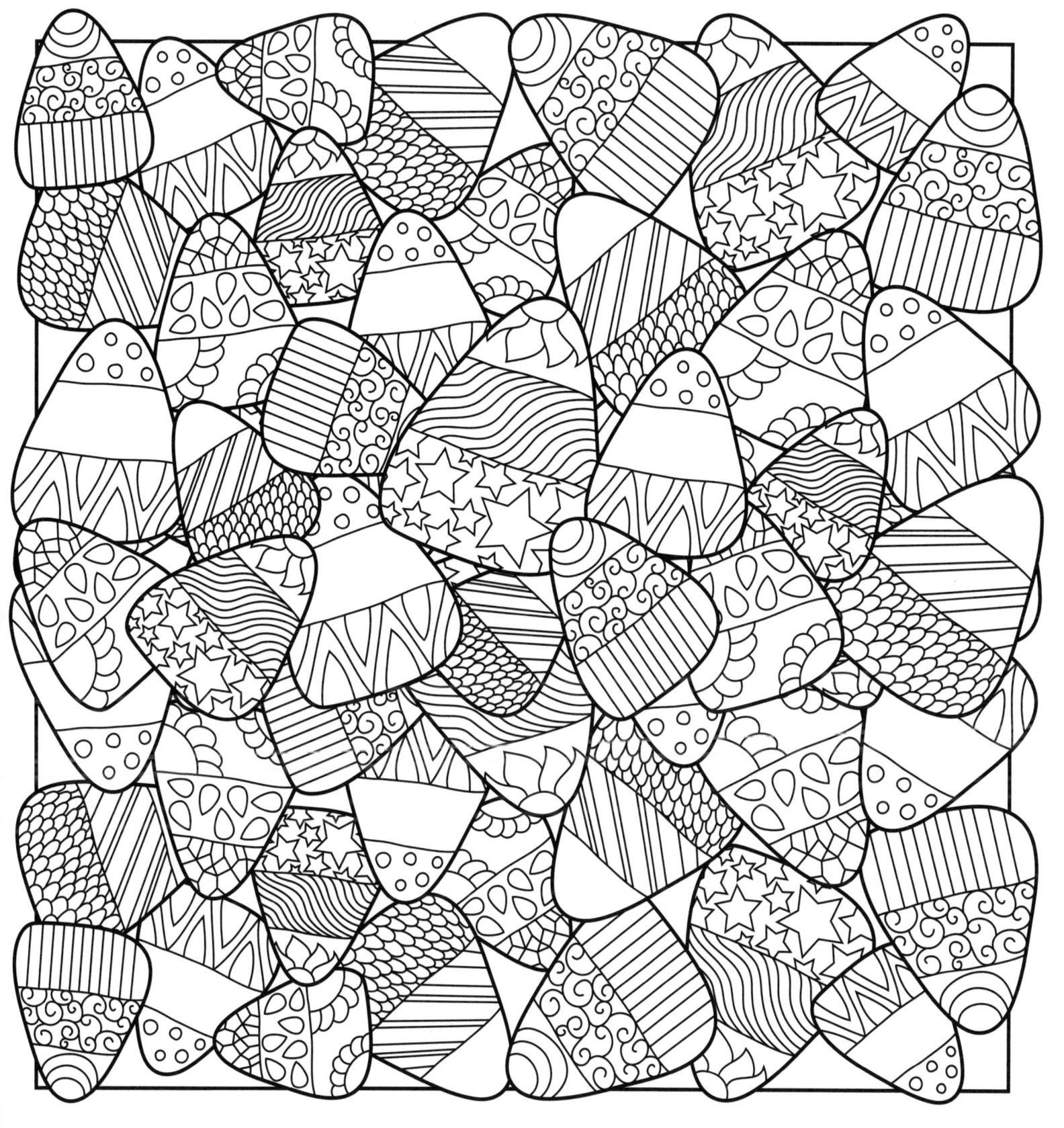

Where there is no imagination there is no horror.

—Arthur Conan Doyle

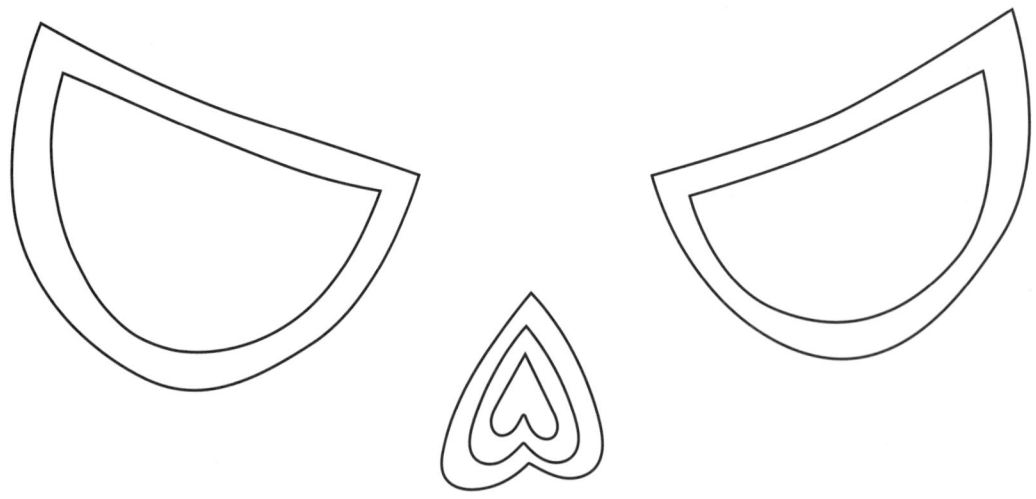

When wild, ugly faces we carved in its skin,
Glaring out through the dark with a candle within!

—John Greenleaf Whittier

And each separate dying ember
wrought its ghost upon the floor.

—Edgar Allan Poe

Oh, when I was a little Ghost,
A merry time had we!

—Lewis Carroll

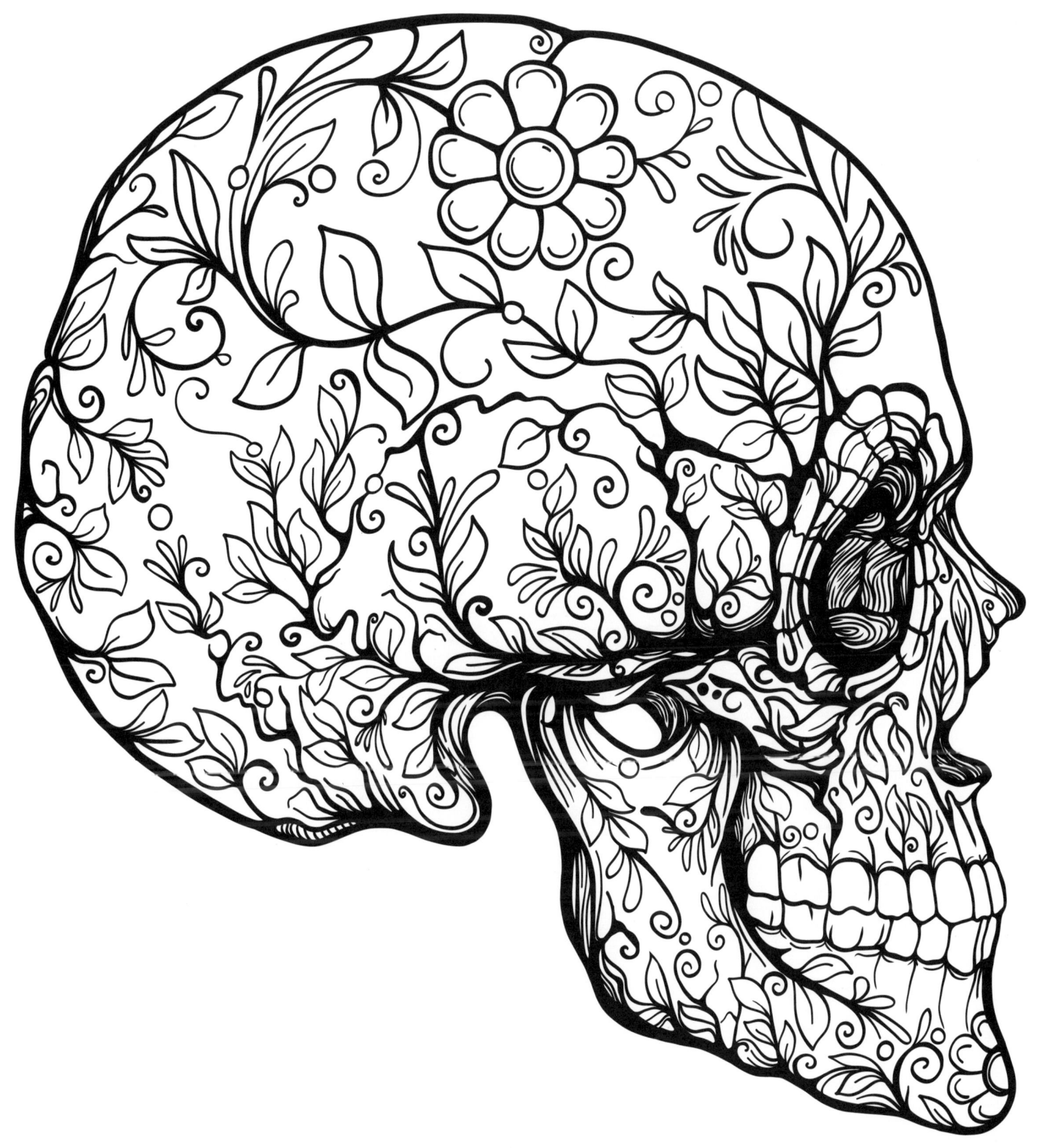

The screech-owl, with ill-boding cry,
Portends strange things.

—Mary Wortley Montagu

STAY SPOOKY

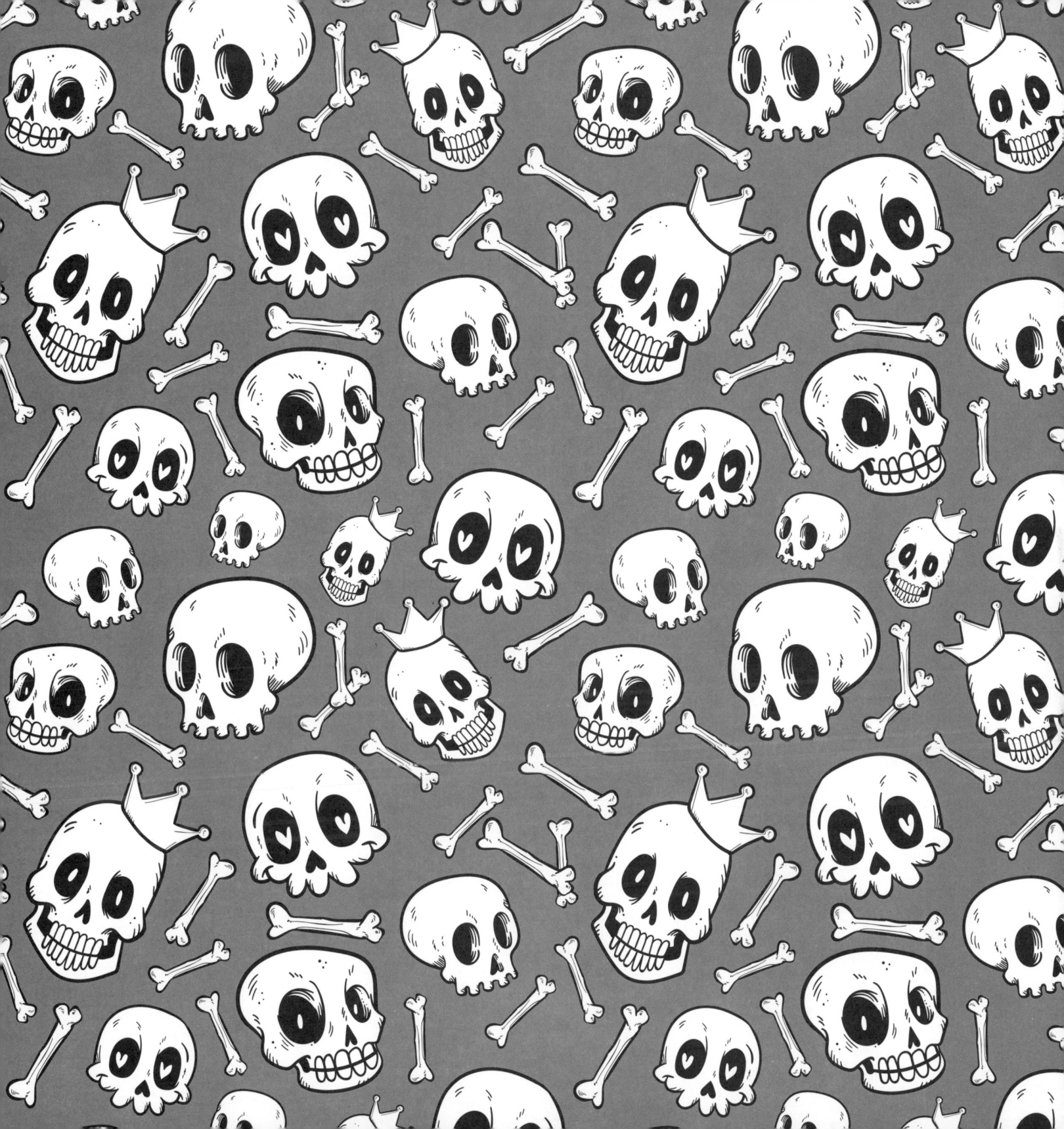

Between me and the moonlight flitted a great bat,
coming and going in great whirling circles.

—Bram Stoker

SPOOK -A- LICIOUS

Whoever is not in his coffin and the dark grave
let him know he has enough.

—Walt Whitman

Life itself is but the shadow of death, and souls departed but the shadows of the living.

–Thomas Browne

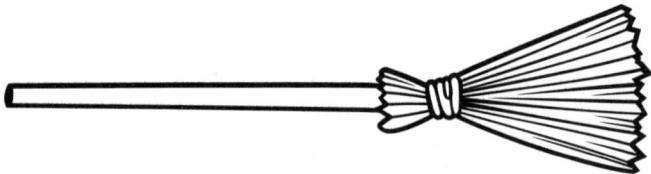

SPOOKTACULAR

Now it is the time of night,
That the graves, all gaping wide,
Every one lets forth his sprite.

—William Shakespeare

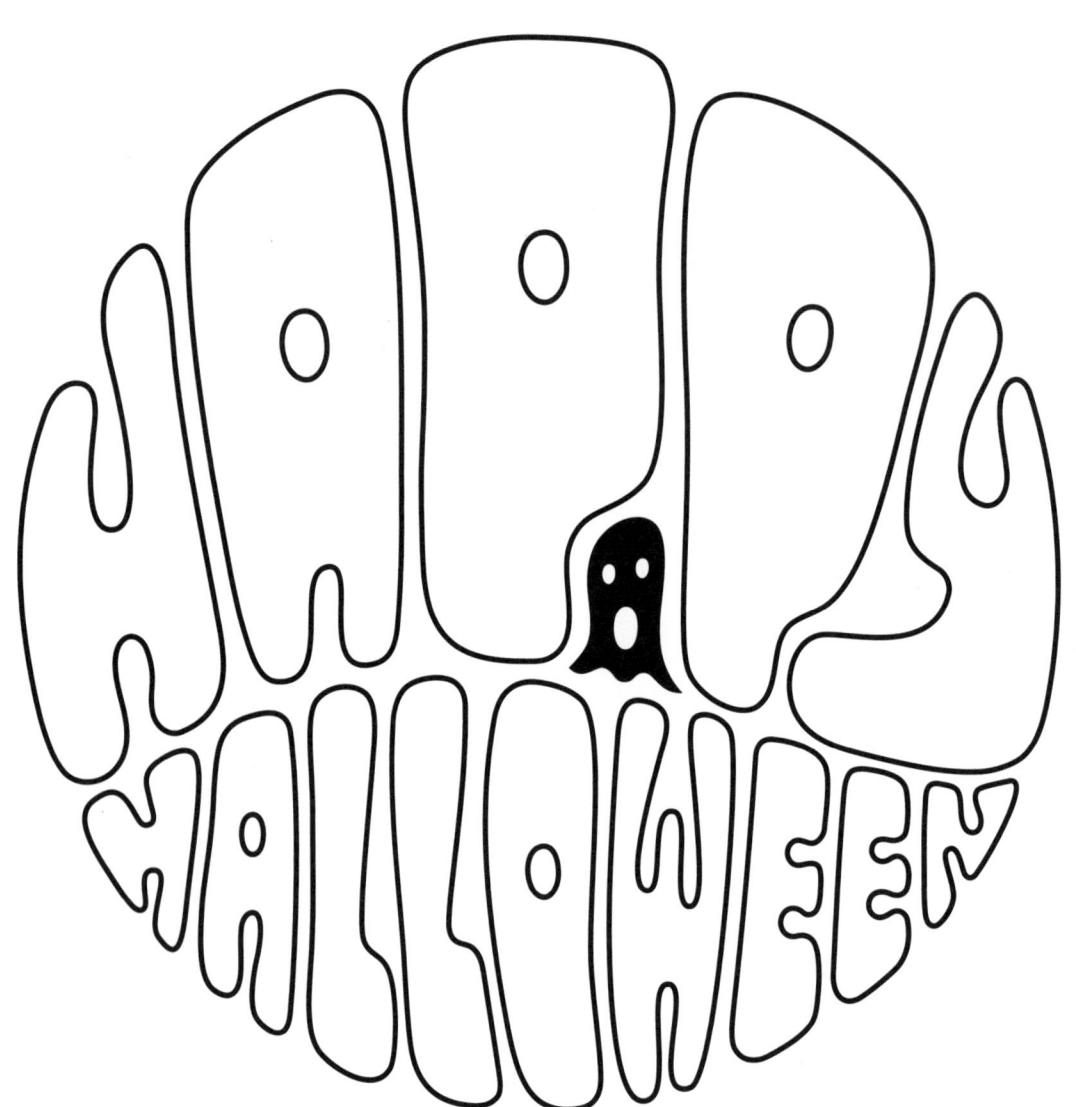

On this night of all nights in the year,
Ah, what demon hath tempted me here?

—Edgar Allan Poe

PEACE LOVE HALLOWEEN

Across the black darkness the windows admitted pale sheeted ghosts of light upon the floor.

—Elizabeth Gaskell

All hope abandon, ye who enter here.

—Dante Alighieri

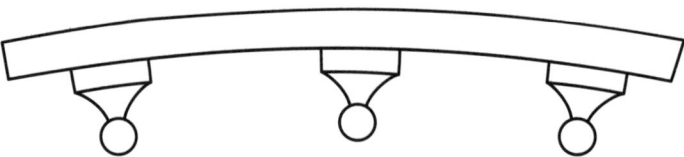

SOMETHING WICKED THIS WAY COMES

There was no moon, and everything beneath lay in misty darkness.

—Emily Brontë

When we laughed round the corn-heap, with hearts all in tune,
Our chair a broad pumpkin,—our lantern the moon.

—John Greenleaf Whittier

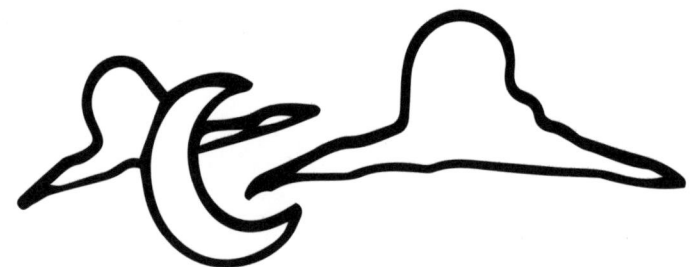

Believe nothing you hear, and only one half that you see.

—Edgar Allan Poe

'Tis the Season to be Spooky

The walls were fluffy and heavy with dust, and in the corners were masses of spider's webs.

—Bram Stoker

Witches weave at night
Their magic spells with impish glee.

—Eugene Field

 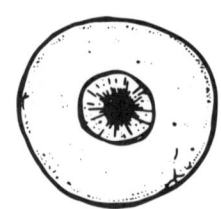

I knew nothing but shadows
and I thought them to be real.

—Oscar Wilde

Yeah I Can Drive a Stick

All these, however, were mere terrors of the night, phantoms of the mind that walk in darkness.

—Washington Irving

Have a BOO-tiful Night

Listen...
With faint dry sound,
Like steps of passing ghosts,
The leaves, frost-crisp'd, break from the trees
And fall.

—Adelaide Crapsey

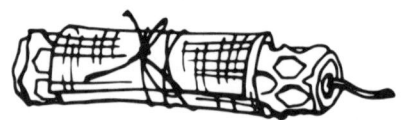

Whatever mystifies, excites curiosity; whatever in turn baffles this curiosity, works the marvelous.

—Alexander Herrmann

I AIN'T afraid OF NO Ghost

I know of the leafy paths that the witches take,
Who come with their crowns of pearl and their spindles of wool.

—W. B. Yeats

ghouls just wanna have fun

From larks and sunlit dreams to owl and gibbering ghost;
A catacomb of dark, a maze of living light.

—Richard Le Gallienne

The trees are in their autumn beauty,
The woodland paths are dry,
Under the October twilight the water
Mirrors a still sky.

—W. B. Yeats

And my soul from out that shadow that lies floating on the floor
Shall be lifted—nevermore!

—Edgar Allan Poe

For a dreamer is one who can only find his way by moonlight.

—Oscar Wilde